The REAL Story of

Pirates

Fun Facts, Tall Tales, and Awesome Activities

REAL STORY
BOOKS
Let Your Imagination Take Flight!

Written, illustrated, and designed by
Gregory B. Edmonds. Copyright © 2018

ISBN-13: 978-0-692-10102-5

Library of Congress Control Number: 2018939932

Real Story Books
Publisher

www.RealStoryBooks.com

REAL STORY
BOOKS
Let Your Imagination Take Flight!

For Tammie, Alex, and Mary

I couldn't have imagined better.

Special Thanks
to Lyle and Trish Brite—without whom this publication would
not have been undertaken—for their invaluable assistance in
researching all of the topics included and for posing and
providing examples of the equipment used
for the illustrations found herein.

contents

NOTES FOR PARENTS

Walt Disney wasn't the first to recognize the fact that most children are fascinated by pirates; many pirate tales were published long before the film industry came along. It can be said, however, that Disney inspired the last six decades of interest in pirating. First came the 1958 film adaptation of the Robert Lewis Stevenson classic *Treasure Island*, which was followed by related titles.

In 1967, *Disneyland* (the original Disney theme park located in Anaheim, California) opened the very first *Pirates of the Caribbean* live-action animatronic character ride. A year later, Disney Studios went on to release the film *Blackbeard's Ghost*. It was in 2003, when the studio launched the hugely successful *Pirates of the Caribbean* film franchise, that pirates became extremely popular all over again with a new generation of children and grown-ups alike.

Recommended Discussion Topics

While the majority of pirates appearing in the Disney (and similar) films are seen as tough but lovable rogues, the fact is, real-life pirates were probably not the kind of folks you would invite to dinner.

Pirates were outlaws, thieves, and (sometimes) killers. There were some, however, who actually worked on what was regarded as the *right side* of law. Among these were the group of sailors known as "privateers." Privateers were, basically, pirates for hire. They assisted the fledgling United States government a number of times and worked for, or on behalf of, a number of other world powers, too.

What does your child think of pirates? Were pirates (or privateers) hired by governments really "bad guys?" How about women pirates? Many don't know that they existed!

Have a look at the popular phrases and idioms that began in the pirating era: *a flash in the pan*, *footloose*, *pipe down*, *by and large* and others, all came from the classic age of pirates and life at sea. A collection of these words and expressions (along with their original meanings) is found in the section called *Do You Talk Like a Pirate?*

Children aged nine and older should enjoy reading this book on their own. Younger children may need help with defining some words as you read with them (there's a glossary on page 66). As the author, I hope this and future books in this series will become a regular part of the time you spend reading with your children and the time they spend reading alone. Future books will cover topics ranging from dinosaurs to astronauts. Reading with young children at bedtime helps promote a life-long interest in learning, vocabulary, and imagination. This book's maze and other activities offer a few brain-stimulating challenges, too.

"Color Me" Pages

Only crayons (and graphite or colored pencils) should be used to write or color on the paper used in this book. I encourage you to make a photocopy (*for personal use only, please*) of each drawing and puzzle so they can be colored or completed separately, leaving the book's pages clean for the next reading.

JB Edmonds

A Brief History of Pirating

A pirate is best described as any person who uses boats, ships, and the seas to commit crimes—especially theft and kidnapping. Piracy has been going on for a very long time and still does today in some parts of the world. The first pirates were known simply as "the Sea People" and they lived around 3,600 years ago. Like pirates who lived much later, they stole property from ships belonging to others. They sometimes stole the ships, too.

When we hear the word "pirate" today, we are usually thinking of the people who lived between the 1500s and about 1830. During that period of time, mariners (sailors) on the tall ships carrying supplies and valuables from one country to another had to constantly be on the look-out for other ships they might see on the horizon. There was a good chance that the ship they saw carried pirates.

As suggested by the titles in the popular movies and theme-park ride produced by Disney, most real pirate activity took place in the Caribbean sea between the years 1660 and 1730. The Caribbean is an area of more than 700 large and small islands, reefs, and caves found east of the Gulf of Mexico and southeast of the area now known as the United States of America.

Buccaneers

Some of the early pirates (also known as "freebooters") in this era were called Buccaneers. They mainly attacked Spanish ships beginning the early 1600s in an area known then as the "West Indies" (which is now called the Caribbean).

Tall Ship

G. Edmonds

Color Me

Many of the original buccaneers were Frenchmen who hunted wild boar and raised cattle, the meat from which was then smoked and prepared as jerky. They started out by selling their products to Corsairs (French privateers), with whom they eventually went into pirating and were joined by both Dutch and English mariners. They were based on the then-mostly uninhabited islands of Tortuga and Hispaniola, in Haiti. The Spanish tried to drive them away from these locations but were unsuccessful. The British government approved of Buccaneers (and the French Corsairs, who eventually went by this name too) because they mostly attacked Spanish ships, when Spain and the British were at war.

The English governor of Jamaica, Thomas Modyford, invited the buccaneers to base their ships on the island of Port Royal. The buccaneers continued to attack Spanish vessels and colonies for decades. British and European governments eventually turned against them, because of their often violent ways. Some Buccaneers not defeated in battle eventually became farmers and peddlers in this region.

Privateers

Privateers were best described as sailors who became pirates for hire. They carried "Letters of Marque," which were basically genuine licenses to steal. These letters were issued by the official government of one nation, like England, who was at war or in a disagreement with another nation, like Spain. The young American colonies also used privateers, some of them freed African slaves, in their struggle for independence.

Crimes like theft, kidnapping, and violence were all permitted by the Letters of Marque possessed by privateering captains. Privateers would split up their stolen profits and valuables amongst themselves and with the governments of the nations or individuals who sponsored them.

Fight or Surrender!

G. Edmonds

Color Me

Pirate Flags

Different pirate ships often displayed different flags. The most famous pirate flag was known as the "Jolly Roger." A few different designs were called by this name, but the most common displayed a skull with crossed bones. Barbary Pirates first used a flag with a skull around 1500.

The famous skull and crossbones design used by pirates Calico Jack and Edward England may have been copies of Barbary flags whose own pirates copied the design from the gravestones of Knights Templar (warriors who served in the Holy Land—modern Israel—in the 12th century).

Other pirate flags included those with an hourglass and darts or daggers. Sometimes the dagger was shown piercing a heart with drops of blood appearing to drip from it. The heart and blood were often colored red. The famous pirate Captain Blackbeard's flag had a skeleton with horns on it (he liked to be thought of as the "son of the devil") as well a spear pointed at a bleeding heart.

Another popular design used by privateers and pirates displayed a skull and swords. "Calico Jack" Rackham was the first to display such a flag, while pirate Thomas Tew used only the symbol of swords on his flag.

All of these flags served the same purpose: they were used as a warning that your ship was about to be boarded by pirates. If you were a ship's captain, when you saw a pirate flag, you had only seconds to decide whether you and your crew would run, fight, or surrender.

Sample Pirate Flags

G. Edmonds

Famous Pirates of the Past

We don't really know exactly how many pirates roamed the seas in the period of time known as the classic or "golden" age of pirating. Nor do we know what the most famous pirates really looked like unless they had drawings made of themselves. When they did appear in artwork, they most often wore fancy clothing like that seen on the cover of this book, including coats with pockets and a tricorn (three-cornered) hat. When they were working, they wore very plain clothing, with no pockets.

Beginning on page 13 are short profiles of some of the more famous pirates and privateers who were active in the centuries between 1520 and about 1830. Some famous privateers went on to have quite successful lives in business and government. We know of them now because they were seen as heroes in the countries for which they worked.

Pirates, on the other hand, very often became famous because they were captured by the nations whose ships they attacked. Drawings of them were sometimes made while they were awaiting trial or execution.

Remember, privateers carried very special papers called *Letters of Marque* which identified them as official representatives of the nations which employed them. These documents usually kept privateers from being arrested (for crimes like theft, kidnapping, and assault) by the nations who issued the letters.

Other countries though (especially those who owned or hired the ships that the privateers attacked) did not recognize these letters. To these countries, privateers were just the same as any other pirate, and if captured, they were put in prison, and more often, hanged.

Barbarossa

Barbarossa (which means "red beard") was a name shared by the pirate brothers Khidr and Aruj, who worked for the Ottoman Empire (now known as Turkey) in its struggle against Spain. Based in Algiers, North Africa, Aurj was eventually killed in battle. His brother Khidr continued to attack Spanish and Portuguese ships as a privateer and went on to become an admiral of the Ottoman Empire around 1520.

Black Bart

"Bartholomew" Roberts, whose given name was actually John, was a pirate from Wales who was best known for raiding ships off the coast of the Americas between the years 1719 and 1722. Originally first mate on a slave ship, Bart was captured by pirates and eventually became one himself. During the last three years of his life, Black Bart successfully attacked over 400 ships, making him the richest pirate of his time. Black Bart is famous for creating what was known as the "Pirate's Code," rules which were honored by many pirates in the years to follow. He died in battle in February of 1722, when he was surprised by the British warship *The Swallow* while in the process of looting a merchant vessel.

Blackbeard

Edward Teach (thought to be the real name of the notorious pirate Blackbeard) was born in England (or possibly South Carolina). He served as a privateer for England's Queen Elizabeth I but then set out on his own, becoming a pirate based in New Providence, The Bahamas. He, along with pirate Stede Bonnet, went to work for pirate Captain Benjamin Hornigold around 1716 and took over when Hornigold retired a year later. Blackbeard captured the French Merchant ship *Queen Anne's Revenge* which he sailed on thereafter. He led a group of other pirates to form a blockade of the port of Charles Town, in

South Carolina, where he held all of the citizens hostage. Shortly after this, he accidentally ran his ship aground (meaning that he got her stuck on a sandbar) off the coast of Beaufort, North Carolina (ships were always called "she" or "her" rather than "it"). He then parted from his fellow pirate captain Stede Bonnet and accepted a royal pardon from the governor of North Carolina. Soon, however, he returned to the sea and to pirating. The governor of Virginia, Alexander Spotswood, paid to have Blackbeard brought to justice. On November 22, 1718, while most of his men were ashore drinking, Blackbeard's ship was attacked. After a fierce battle in which he was reportedly shot five times and stabbed or slashed 11 times, the greatly feared pirate Captain Blackbeard died of his wounds.

Stede Bonnet

Captain Stede Bonnet, an associate of the famous pirate Blackbeard, was a native of Barbados, in the Caribbean. He was known as "the gentleman pirate" because he was a well-to-do landowner before becoming a pirate (he inherited his wealth from his English family). In 1717, he turned to a life of crime at sea after having money troubles and the reported break-up of his marriage. He hired a crew of pirates and together they raided ships along the east coast of the Americas and burned ships from Barbados. He met Blackbeard in Nassau, The Bahamas, after having been wounded in battle. Like Blackbeard, he was eventually given a full pardon by North Carolina Governor Charles Eden. Although he, too, returned to pirating, he still kept his official pardon papers. He was nonetheless eventually captured by Colonel William Rhett on the orders of South Carolina's Governor Robert Johnson. At trial, Captain Bonnet was sentenced to death but was able to briefly avoid his fate by escaping from custody. He was recaptured only days later and hanged in Charles Town (now Charleston) on December 10, 1718.

Woman Pirate

G. Edmonds

Color Me

15

Anne Bonny

Anne Bonny was a female pirate operating in the Caribbean in the 1700s. She was born in Kinsale County, Ireland, and was the daughter of a servant woman. William Cormac, her father, for whom her mother worked, left Anne's mother and moved with Anne to London. There, he dressed Anne like a boy and began calling her "Andy." Anne's father eventually reunited with her mother, and moved with them to Charles Town, South Carolina. Anne was reported to have a terrible temper. She married a poor sailor named James Bonny, against the wishes of her father, who then disinherited her. She set her father's plantation on fire as revenge and then moved on to Nassau, in The Bahamas. She eventually became a partner (both pirate and romantic) of Calico Jack Rackham, who was captain of the tall ship *Revenge*. As she did when she was a child, Anne once again pretended to be a boy while on Rackham' ship. Anne was imprisoned in 1720 but later released, it is currently unknown what eventually became of her. No record of her death appears to exist.

Calico Jack

Pirate Capitan Jack Rackham, known as "Calico Jack" because of the calico fabric in the clothing he wore, was active near the end of the "golden age" of piracy. Not much is known about Calico Jack's birth or upbringing. Among his crew were Anne Bonny as well as another female pirate named Mary Read. Jack's first mate, a man named Karl Starling, adopted the often-copied skull and crossbones Jolly Roger flag. Captain Jack eventually replaced the bones on the flag with crossed swords. Although his name is well-known today, Calico Jack was really not a very successful pirate. He and his crew did not fight well, and they never gathered very much wealth. Jack mainly attacked and plundered smaller merchant ships. He was captured when his crew members were drinking ashore in Jamaica, and later executed in November of 1720.

Sir Francis Drake

Francis Drake was an English Sea Captain and slave trader who (like Blackbeard) served as a privateer for Queen Elizabeth I. He was famous for his expeditions to discover new lands and claim them in the name of England. The Queen awarded him a knighthood in 1581 for his years of maritime service to his country. As a privateer, he led many attacks on Spanish ships. In Spain, he was known as a pirate (this was often the case for privateers who served an opposing government) and Spain's King Philip II offered a reward of 20,000 ducats for his capture and death—that's more than eight million American dollars, today. Sir Francis Drake was also active in politics in his lifetime. He served as a member of the British Parliament and worked on many important topics of his day. Drake's reputation suffered when he took part in an incident known as the Rathlin Island Massacre in which 600 people were killed after they had surrendered. Although he was active in sea battles against the Spanish until near the very end of his life, Sir Francis eventually died of the then-common disease called dysentery on January 28, 1596, just shortly before his 56th birthday.

Captain Kidd

William Kyd (later spelled Kidd) was a Scottish mariner born in the mid-1600s. After his father died at sea, another local family supported him as he grew up. Captain Kidd settled in New York City, and is believed to have served as an apprentice seaman on a pirate vessel. While later serving on a pirate ship in the Caribbean, Kidd mutinied with other crewman and took over the ship. He was famous for attacking the French-held island of Marie-Galante, where he and his crew took over 2,000 pounds Sterling (silver coin). He later married a wealthy New York widow and went on to serve as a privateer. He avoided piracy against his sponsors, but was eventually accused of great acts of cruelty including torturing prisoners and killing a member of his own crew after an argument. Most of the crimes for which Captain Kidd was charged were actually committed by his crew. On one occasion, he made his crew members return items which had been stolen from a merchant ship called *The Mary*, which they had ransacked against Britain's wishes. Kidd was formally accused of being a pirate by an officer of the British Royal Navy. His crew members finally stopped taking his orders altogether, and refused to return items looted from another ship (also under British protection) operated by the East Indian Trading Company. Though they eventually abandoned him, Kidd was charged with piracy mostly because of the actions of the crew he could not control. He was tricked by an investor named Bellomont (himself afraid of being tried for piracy) who turned Kidd over to authorities after luring him to Boston. Captain Kidd was arrested on July 6, 1699, and placed in solitary confinement in Stone Prison. His wife was also put in jail. Kidd was sent to England a year later and questioned by members of Parliament. He finally stood trial at the High Court of the Admiralty, charged with piracy and murder, and found guilty of all charges. He was hanged on May 23, 1701.

Sir Henry Morgan

Henry Morgan was a Welsh privateer and landowner who later served as Lieutenant Governor of Jamaica, where he was based at Port Royal. Morgan raided Spanish ships and settlements and became wealthy from the properties looted in those activities. After the British signed a peace treaty with Spain, Morgan attacked property held by the Spanish in Panama, South America. Because of Spain's anger over this incident, Morgan was arrested and taken to London. After arriving there, he was actually treated as a hero and eventually set free. He died, at age 53, in Lawrencefield, Jamaica, of natural causes. Today, a very popular brand of rum is named for Captain Morgan.

Flintlock Pistol

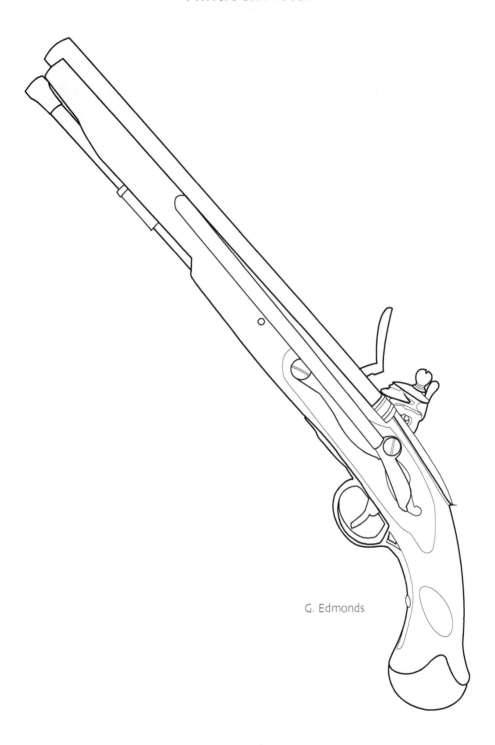

G. Edmonds

Color Me

19

Fact *or* Tall Tale?

British Admiral Edward Vernon (known as "Old Grogram") ordered that a mixture of water and rum be given to the men of the Royal Navy while they were at sea. The drink was first named "grog," after the admiral's grogram-cloth coat, in 1770. Grog was offered to British sailors for the next 200 years. When on land, mariners would visit public houses (now called "pubs" or "bars") where they would be served pure rum. To be sure that they were getting what they paid for, the sailors were said to conduct an experiment on the rum called "proofing."

To proof the rum, a little of it was spilled on a plate or table and a small sprinkle of gunpowder added to the edge of the puddle. If the powder and the liquid both burned when exposed to high temperatures, a sailor knew that he had 100 percent rum with a high alcohol content. This is said to be where the word "proof," which is found on liquor bottles today, comes from.

Burning tobacco ash from a sailor's pipe might be used to ignite the mixture. Some smaller items a sailor used for this purpose—which might be carried in a "possibles bag" (illustrated on page 30)—are seen on the facing page.

The long teardrop-shaped glass object pictured is a another kind of powder horn (described on page 26). Because the glass horn could break, it might not be carried into battle. It was, however, was much easier to see how much powder was left inside the transparent container.

Sailor's Personal Items

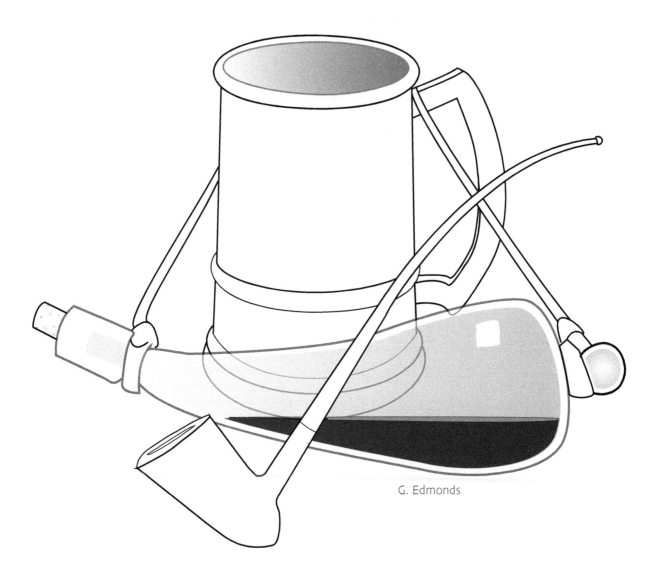

G. Edmonds

Color Me

Equipment Used by Pirates

In the golden age of pirates, there were no engines like today and of course no satellites, computers, or electronic maps. Tall ships were only powered by the wind, which was collected in their large sails.

Naturally, you wouldn't just climb aboard a ship and let the winds take you wherever you might end up. That's why even the most basic tools and techniques for navigation were so very important. In the early days, pirates guided their ships by knowing the position of the stars and constellations in the night sky and by knowing where the four corners of the compass were (by watching the sun rise and set). In later times an instrument called the sextant was used for the purpose of navigating the ship.

One of the early instruments used to help show a ship's position on the ocean was called a backstaff. Seen on page 25 (behind the compass rose) the backstaff was used to measure how high or low an object in the sky—like the moon—was compared to the line of the horizon. By using this device, plus knowing his direction on the compass and the time of day or night, a mariner could tell roughly where he was on the sea. While both large and small sails powered tall ships, they were steered by a device called the rudder, which was at the rear (or aft) portion of the vessel, attached to the bottom. When the ship's wheel was turned in a given direction, ropes and pulleys between the wheel and the rudder would be pulled one way or the other, causing the ship to turn on the water's surface.

The wind did not always cooperate and blow in the direction the ship's captain and his crew wanted to go. When this happened, the sails were repositioned and the upright position of the ship (called the roll) changed

Steering the Ship

G. Edmonds

Color Me

using the wheel, so that the wind might be captured on the favorable side of the sails. Before the development of the compass and sextant, a ship's location and direction were determined by the use of simple objects like a "loadstone," which was a magnetic rock. Repeatedly rubbing the tip of a small iron needle against a loadstone caused the needle to become magnetized. When placed on a thin sliver of wood in a cup of shallow water, the floating needle's tip would point north.

An instrument called the "astrolabe" was developed in the early 15th century. An astrolabe contained specially marked circular dials which could be lined up against either the sun or a known star; these would help provide the star's altitude (height) against the horizon line. In combination with a compass (or needle magnetized by a loadstone), the astrolabe was used to tell where a ship was located in the sea and make it possible to plot the correct course or direction of travel.

Another device, called the "Diptych Dial," was used to calculate both time and a ship's direction. It contained two sections (called leaves), one of which was upright, and the other which lay flat, and a built-in compass. By lining up a hole on the upright leaf with the sun, a sailor was able to roughly determine the time and his position by watching the shadow of a string move on the dial's (flat) etched lower leaf.

A ship's speed, which is measured in "knots" (a term still used by both mariners and aircraft pilots), was determined by the following process. A length of rope, with knots tied along it at equal distances, had a piece of weighted wood (called a "chip log") on one end. The chip log was tossed into the sea and dragged behind the vessel. The rope was anchored to a reel aboard the ship, which was let out at a timed interval as measured by a small hourglass every half minute.

A Backstaff (in the rear) and a Compass Rose

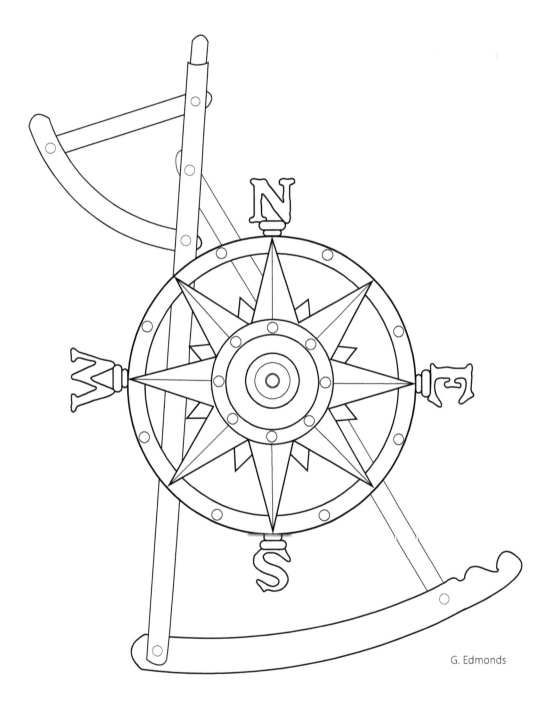

G. Edmonds

Color Me

The number of rope knots that passed through the mariners' hands during these brief periods was used to calculate how fast the ship was going in "knots per hour." One mile per hour equals .87 knots, and one kilometer per hour equals .54 knots.

Weapons were the most important pieces of equipment a pirate had to carry into battle. Choice weapons included flintlock firearms. Flintlocks worked much the same as modern rifles and pistols in that a small explosion of gunpowder caused a metal object (much like a modern bullet) to be projected through a barrel outward toward a target. Unlike such weapons of today, however, the projectiles (balls) used in flintlocks were not enclosed in a shell or cartridge. To operate a flintlock pistol (or rifle), the pirate had to pour a very carefully measured amount of powder into the weapon's barrel using a special measuring tube (seen on the facing page). The gunpowder was kept in a powder horn, which was made from a real hollowed-out animal horn that was sealed at one end and had a removable plug at the other.

Tools used with the flintlock included a long straight pin (or prick) used for clearing the vent hole between the "pan" (where a spark was ignited) and the powder (which was in the gun's barrel—see drawing on page 35). After the powder was poured into the barrel, a ramrod was used to pack it in place behind a small piece of cloth. This was followed by a metal ball, which was then jammed into place and held by the piece of cloth inside the barrel. When the trigger was pulled a spark was ignited after a piece of flint struck the frizzen (striking plate) which would cause the powder in the pan and that packed inside of the barrel to explode and send the metal ball within on its way. Flintlocks were deadly weapons, and some pirates carried several of them at once, because of the time they took to reload in battle. Hunters used flintlocks on land.

Flintlock Tools and Boatswain's (or Bosun's) Pipe

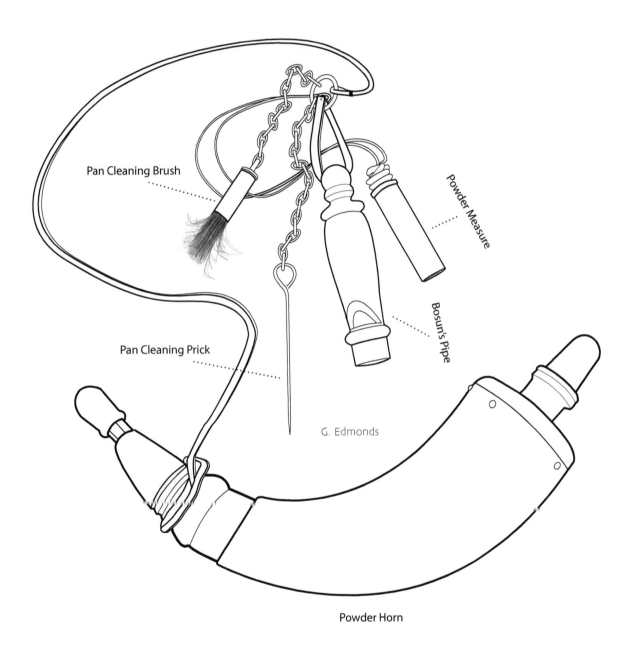

Pan Cleaning Brush

Powder Measure

Bosun's Pipe

Pan Cleaning Prick

G. Edmonds

Powder Horn

Color Me

Not every pirate and Navy crew member was able to carry firearms, which could cost a lot of money. All, however, were usually equipped with edged weapons like swords and knives.

There were different kinds of swords such as a cutlasses (which were slightly curved) and sabers (swords with thicker curved blades, which were sharpened only on a single edge), and rapiers (with thin blades, used for slashing and stabbing). Most knives and swords were kept in protective leather holders called scabbards (as seen on the facing page). A pirate's ability to fight with a sword and knife might well determine whether he or she lived or died in battle.

Hatchets, battle axes, and regular knives might also be used in working aboard a ship for cutting the lines (ropes) during storms and battles, as well as for use in carpentry and woodworking.

Dirks, darts, and daggers were smaller swords or knives with very sharp points that were often carried into battle. Some could be hidden in a tricorn hat, inside a shirt, or up a sleeve, and were designed for use as either stabbing or throwing weapons. Such weapons were most often carried constantly by pirates and frequently by other mariners.

Large cannons, which fired eight-pound balls of iron, were used against mostly land-based target like walls or buildings. They were hard to manipulate and required several crew members to operate in battle. Smaller type cannons might fire chains, bars, or grapeshot (a collection of smaller metal balls) and were usually used to take out a ship's masts or sails. If an opponent's ship sank, no booty could be collected. Swivel guns were often mounted on a ship's command or quarterdeck, and could be used against an enemy or to discourage mutiny.

Cutlass and Dagger

G. Edmonds

Color Me

A "Possibles Bag," used to carry tools, extra flint, shot and other items.

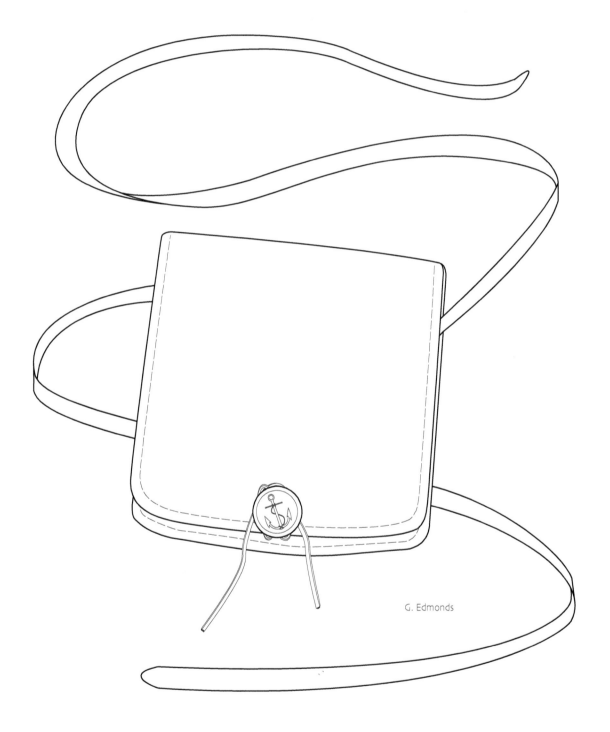

G. Edmonds

Color Me

Hatchet and Long Knife

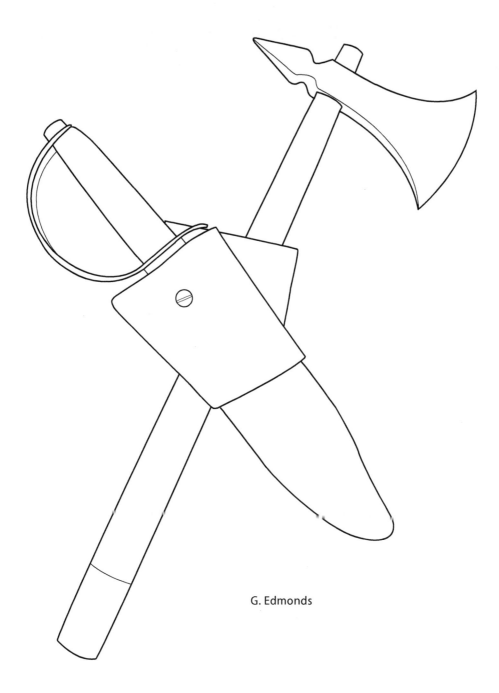

G. Edmonds

Color Me

Fact or Tall Tale?

In the days of pirates, young men sometimes became mariners because they thought the idea of working on a ship and living on the sea sounded exciting. Sometimes, they became sailors because they could find no other work.

More than a few such men were forced to work on ships, whether they wanted to, or not. When a government made you work for its navy, the process was called "conscription." When both pirate and naval ships needed extra crewmen, they might "press" unwilling sailors into service. Some were kidnapped at gunpoint and forced to go aboard a ship. At other times, shipping companies (and pirates) might secretly slip a drug into a sailor's mug, while he was sitting in a pub, which made him go to sleep. The victim would wake up aboard a ship on which he did not wish to serve. This was known as being "shanghaied."

Some say the British Navy would try to trick mariners into coming aboard. When a sailor wasn't looking, a bartender might slip a shilling coin into the mug or tankard from which the sailor was sipping. If he accepted the cup with the coin, the Navy claimed that the sailor had been "paid" and so "agreed" to serve on the ship. Some sailors carried glass-bottomed mugs (or tankards) so they could see that no coin had been slipped inside before drinking.

Glass-bottomed Tankard

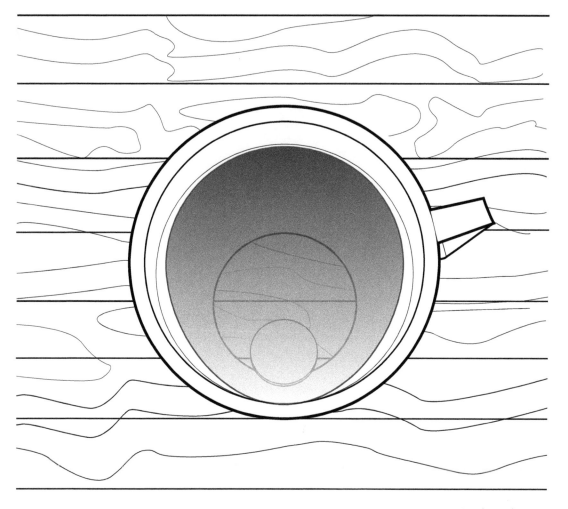

G. Edmonds

Color Me

Do You Talk Like a Pirate?

Every year since 2002, on September 19th, many English-speaking people take part in the "International Talk Like a Pirate Day." On this date, it is not uncommon to hear (especially on radio stations and local TV shows) media personalities and everyday people saying things like "avast," "aye, matey," and "argh" (which sounds like the letter R stretched out over several seconds). Many people think pirates really talked this way. In reality, they did not.

British actor Robert Newton, who played the role of pirate Long John Silver in the Disney movie *Treasure Island,* and who revisited the character in other films, was the first to introduce this way of speaking. His style of pronouncing words was immediately copied by people who liked the sound, and it still is today.

What did pirates in the "golden age" really talk like and what words did they use? The best way to understand and copy the words they used is probably to have a look at the original King James version of the Holy Bible. Words like "thee" and "thou" (meaning "you") were often used in the late 15th and early 16th centuries. If you look at the kinds of words used in the earliest papers written by the Founders of the United States (documents like the Declaration of Independence), you get a better idea of what pirates talked like at the end of the classic pirating era.

The word "mariner" is just another name for a sailor or one who works on ships at sea. Lots of words and phrases used by pirates and other mariners are found on the list that begins on the following page. Many of these expressions have different meanings today.

Parts of a Flintlock Pistol

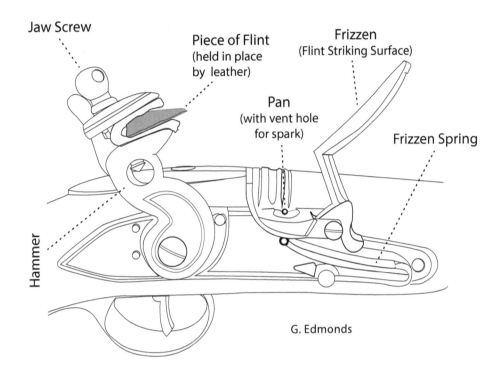

Jaw Screw

Piece of Flint
(held in place
by leather)

Frizzen
(Flint Striking Surface)

Pan
(with vent hole
for spark)

Frizzen Spring

Hammer

G. Edmonds

Flash in the Pan: Today, this expression commonly refers to someone who (or something that) very briefly appears to be promising but turns out to just be of momentary interest. As seen the diagram above, the original term referred to the "pan" part of flintlock firearm where a spark was ignited by a piece of flint (or other stone), shaving off a very tiny piece of metal on the "frizzen" or striking surface when the trigger was pulled. The spark caused gunpowder, which was in the pan and on the other side of the little vent hole in the barrel, to instantly catch fire and explode. This small explosion sent the iron ball out of the gun and toward the target. When the powder ignited but the ball didn't leave the barrel, you had what was known as "a flash in the pan." This situation of course could be very embarrassing in battle!

Three Sheets in the Wind: Today, when we say someone is "three sheets in the wind," we usually mean that they've had too much alcohol to drink. In the original meaning, "sheet lines" were ropes used to control the large sheets of square sails that collected most of the wind's energy on a moving ship. Tall ships often had three of these main square sheets of sail. If the line was not kept taut (tight), the sheets of sail would just flap in the wind, making them useless.

Toe the Line: In modern times, this expression means to follow the rules or regulations in a given situation exactly. In pirate and early modern sailing days, to toe the line meant to stand at attention as a member of the ship's crew, with every crew members' toes touching the same line on the planks of a ship's deck.

Over a Barrel: The expression today refers to being in a difficult situation. Originally, the term "over a barrel" literally meant to be bent over a cannon barrel or ship's grating and being flogged (whipped).

To Know the Ropes: "Knowing the ropes" now means that a person has a good knowledge of his or her profession or excellent job skills. In pirate times, "knowing the ropes" literally meant that everyone aboard the ship knew how to keep track of the many lines (ropes) that were connected to the ship's sails and other moving parts.

Footloose: Today, you might hear the expression "footloose and fancy free," which means that a person doesn't have many responsibilities. On a sailing ship, the term "footloose" simply referred to the foot (bottom-most part) of a sail. If this bit of sail was not tied down, it was free to dance about in the wind.

First Rate: In modern times, the expression "first rate" refers to either a person or thing that is considered very good or the best in its class. You might be a "first rate" ball player. In the 1500s, the term referred to a large sailing ship, especially in the British Royal Navy, that contained 100 or more deck guns. A second-rate ship had 90 to 99 guns, a third-rate ship held 64 to 89 guns, a fourth-rate vessel carried 50 to 63 guns, and a small frigate carrying 48 guns was considered fifth-rate.

Pipe Down: Today, when someone says "pipe down," they are telling you to stop talking. In pirate days the term referred to the very last bosun's pipe signal blown at night. The bosun (sometimes spelled *boatswain*) was in charge of a ship's crew. His "pipe down" was the pipe (whistle) sound that told everyone to put out the lamp lights and go to sleep.

Windfall: Today when you hear someone had a "windfall," it means that they suddenly received a lot of money. The words originally referred to a sudden and unexpected gust of wind that would fill all the ship's sails and move it rapidly forward.

Groggy: Grog was a drink named for British Admiral Edward Vernon, who wore a suit made of a *grogram* (a kind of rough silk fabric, also seen as gros gram). Grog was served to sailors aboard British war ships. It was a mixture of rum and water (usually about half of each) to which lime was sometimes added. To "be groggy" meant to become a little drunk. Today, when someone becomes groggy, it similarly means that they are feeling dazed, sleepy, or unsteady on their feet.

Skyscraper: Today, a skyscraper is a tall building. Originally, a the term identified the highest sail on a ship.

Dressing Down: Today "dressing down" means that someone is firmly correcting you for having made a mistake. In pirate times, "dressing down" referred to rubbing on oil or wax to treat old, worn-out sail cloth. It sometimes had the same basic meaning as today, in that it meant being scolded.

Booby Hatch: In modern times, "bobby hatch" is a way of escaping a bad situation. Originally, a booby (or boobie) hatch was a sliding cover that allowed access to areas beneath a ship's upper decks.

Leeway: The expression today means to be given a little extra freedom to act or move around. Originally, leeway referred to the sideways slip of a ship towards the shore. The wind blows against the ship's "lee" side.

Pooped: Today, when someone says they are "pooped," it generally means that they are very tired. In pirate days, being pooped was very dangerous. The poop deck was the highest deck on a ship. To be "pooped" meant that a large ocean wave or swell had crashed over the poop deck, which could easily have washed any pirate or sailor aboard out to sea.

As the Crow Flies: Now when we say "as the crow flies," we are speaking of the shortest distance between two points on a map. For example, it might be only a few hundred yards or meters as "the crow flies," to your friend's house. If you drive there on the curved roads, however, the distance might be half a mile or a kilometer away. Originally, mariners lost at sea might release a crow from the "crow's nest" (the highest platform on the ship). The freed bird would, hopefully, follow its instincts and fly toward the nearest shore, showing the captain which way to go.

The Crow's Nest - The Highest Platform on a Ship

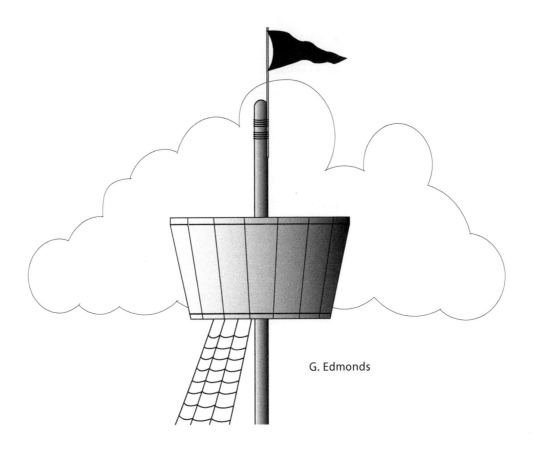

G. Edmonds

By and Large: Today, when people say "by and large," they mean "as a rule," or "in any case." The old nautical term referred to sailing either with the wind (by) or against the wind (large). If the wind blew in both directions on your journey, you were said to be sailing "by and large."

Cut and Run: In modern times, to "cut and run" means to make the best of a bad situation by quitting while you're ahead. When ships met an enemy or pirate vessel during pirate times, to "cut and run" meant to either cut the anchor rope or cut the lines holding up the folded sails. You then "ran" with the wind to get away.

Overhaul: Today, when someone says "overhaul," they're probably talking about a complete rebuilding of something (like a car engine). The term originally referred to the practice of climbing up a ship's masts and pulling the ropes called "bunt" lines over the tops of the crossbars (called "yards" or yard arms) from which the sails were hanging. This kept the lines from rubbing against, and thus ruining, the sails' fabric.

Bear Down: Today, the expression means to physically push harder or to more strongly concentrate attention, or to press harder against an object. A parent might say to you, "bear down and get your homework finished." In pirate times, "bearing down" referred to sailing rapidly toward another ship.

Above Board: The expression today refers to being completely honest, or "forthcoming." The term was originally used to describe the open area above a ship's upper deck (above the boards).

Square Meal: When your parent wants to be sure you eat a "square meal" they mean that it should be well-balanced and have the right amount of food from each food group. A square meal originally referred to the shape of the platters on which mariners' meals were served aboard ship. The platters were square or rectangular in shape so that they fit together and were less likely to slide around on the dinner table when a ship was moving on rough seas.

Fly by Night: In modern times, if someone says a person or business is "fly by night" they mean the one being talked about cannot be trusted. In pirate days, "fly by night" was a term applied to downwind sails, which required little or no attention, especially at night.

No Great Shakes: In modern times, the expression "no great shakes" is used to describe something that isn't very impressive. In old sailing days, it meant the process of tearing apart empty wooden flasks (small barrels) which were found to be empty by shaking.

Touch and Go: Today, when someone says "touch and go," they are describing a situation in which the outcome is uncertain (the condition of a person in the hospital might be referred to as "touch and go"). The term originally referred to a situation in which a ship's rudder (its underwater steering mechanism) touched bottom and then came free again. A stuck rudder was a very bad thing.

Scuttlebutt: This funny word isn't heard very much anymore but it usually means gossip. In the era of pirates, the word "butt" referred to a barrel. Scuttlebutt was a water barrel from which sailors got their drinks. Like now, the term also referred to the discussions, or gossip, they shared, when stopping to dip fresh water.

Pressed into Service: When a person is "pressed into service," sometimes not entirely by choice, they are asked to do a job or perform a task they hadn't originally intended to complete. In pirate times, the term had the same basic meaning, but was more serious. If you were "pressed into service" it meant that you were forced to join the military unit or serve aboard a Navy or pirate ship. Sometimes tricks were used to accomplish the "pressing." See pages 30 and 31 for an example.

Garbled: Today "garbled" usually means a mixed-up message. The word originally referred to letting trash (rubbish) get mixed in with any cargo that a ship was carrying.

Can You find the Treasure?

Almost everyone has heard of a pirate's treasure chest, and a few pirates actually had them.

Gold bars and coins called pieces-of-eight were not the only items hoarded by pirates (as discussed in detail on page 44). They also took many other kinds of "booty" (valuable goods), sometimes even complete ships.

When pirates did steal the kinds of treasure kept in a chest, they sometimes (though *very* rarely) hid it on one of the hundreds of small islands in the Caribbean sea. The treasure would be carefully hidden, very often from other pirates.

Treasure chests (about the size of modern military foot-lockers) were not very large; they had to be small enough for one man to carry. Metal items, especially gold and silver, were very heavy. A larger chest full of treasure would have been impossible to move without help. On the facing page is a maze that leads to a chest full of gold and silver coins, pearls, and other valuables.

Using a pencil with an eraser, take your time and draw a path to the center of the maze so that the treasure in the chest can be yours. Once you get to the treasure, you'll have to find your way out of the maze. Be careful not to cross any lines on your journey. Begin where it says "enter here" and leave where it says "exit here."

Good luck!

Pirate Treasure Maze

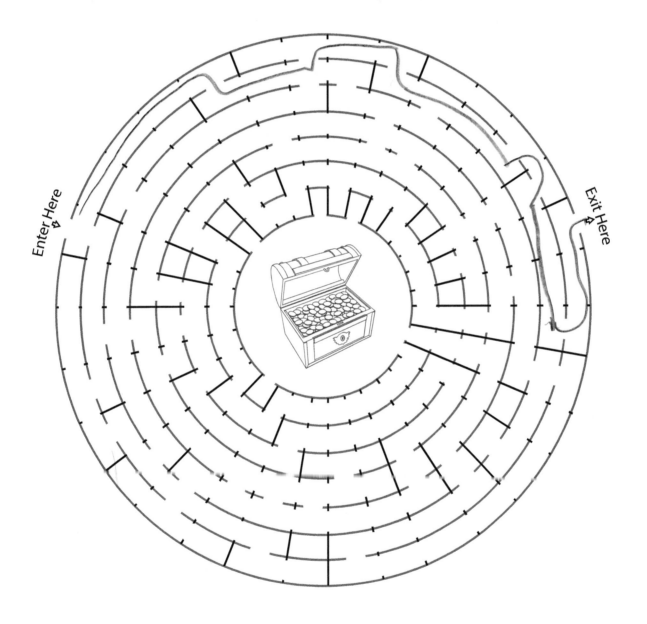

Enter Here

Exit Here

The solution to this maze is found on page 62.

Pirate's Treasure

As discussed on previous pages, most pirates really did share in the stolen treasure from the ships and communities they attacked. What was meant by "treasure," however, might was not necessarily mean the jewels, coins, or the bars of silver and gold sometimes found today at the sites of old shipwrecks. Many things stolen by pirates were *perishable items* like food, spices, wine, rum or ale (beer). While there were a very few cases in which pirates did hide their treasure by burying it on uncharted or little-visited islands, it was not a good idea to bury items that you might later want to eat or drink because they would likely go bad in damp island soil.

A pirate's treasure map can be found on the facing page. Those who followed the "pirate's code" created by Captain "Black Bart" Roberts agreed not to steal from one another. Still, could a pirate really be trusted? Many did mutiny (or take a share and leave) only to join another pirate ship and crew. So, when a pirate drew a map, he hoped no one else would ever see it. In case someone did, he might have pretended that danger existed in the area where the treasure was located. He might even have deliberately marked the wrong burial place for the treasure on his map so the exact spot where the treasure was hidden could never be found. If you look for this island, be sure to watch out for sharks and sea monsters!

G. Edmonds

Pirate Treasure Map

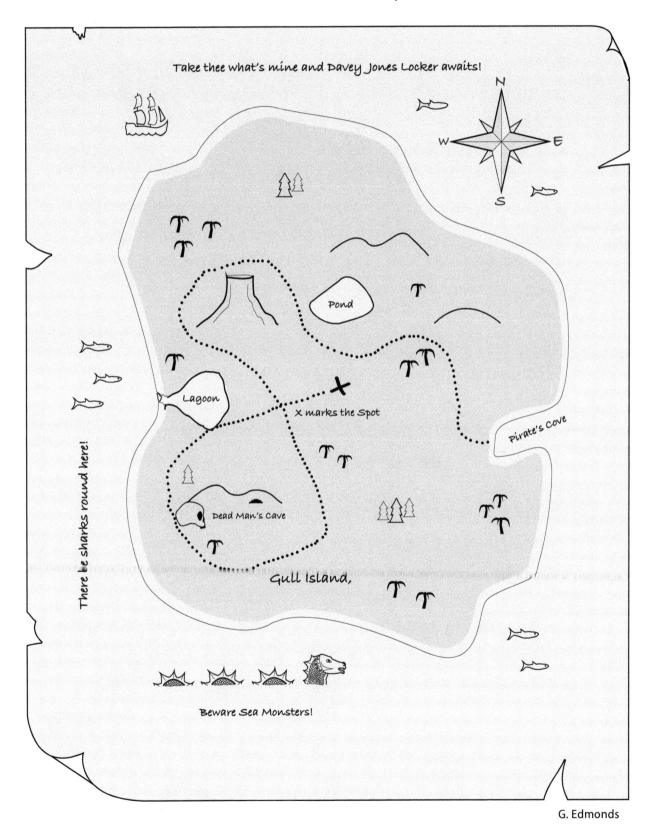

Take thee what's mine and Davey Jones Locker awaits!

Pond

Lagoon

X marks the Spot

Pirate's Cove

Dead Man's Cave

There be sharks round here!

Gull Island,

Beware Sea Monsters!

G. Edmonds

Fact or Tall Tale?

On these pages are questions or statements that may or may not be true. Read them, decide whether you think the statement is correct or not, and then circle whether you believe that it's *True* or *False?*

1. Ironically, the pirate known as Black Bart was actually a religious man. He did not drink any alcohol but allowed his crew to do so. He even held regular Sunday morning church services for members of his crew.
True or *False?*

2. Some mariners were kidnapped when their ships were taken by pirates. These people were sometimes forced to become pirates themselves, or could choose to die instead.
True or *False?*

3. When members of a pirate crew misbehaved or when others who were captured by pirates refused to do as their captors told them, they were often left at sea after being forced to "walk the plank." The plank was a long, wide, board normally used for getting on and off the ship when it was docked or when it came alongside another ship. Pirates frequently made people "walk the plank."
True or *False?*

Answers to these True or False questions are found on page 63.

4. You may have been told that putting your elbows on the dinner table is rude. In pirate times, there was an entirely different reason for sailors to keep their elbows off of the table while visiting pubs on dry land.

True or False?

5. Pirates and privateers often fairly shared the goods they took from others, with the ship's captain getting the most. Many pirates also often buried the treasure they were awarded in the sand on uncharted islands.

True or False?

6. Although many of them had little or no schooling, some people aboard a ship in the pirate era were fully trained in the science of astronomy.

True or False?

7. The disease called scurvy, which caused the gums to rot, the teeth to fall out, and infection to set in, was prevented by putting lime juice in the mixed drink called Grog that was served to sailors. Grog was (usually) made from equal parts rum and fresh water (which was stored on barrels aboard ship). British Royal Navy and pirate ship captains really did give this beverage to their crewmen.

True or False?

Answers to these True or False questions are found on page 64.

Can *You* be the Lookout?

One of the most important jobs on any ship was that of the lookout. The lookout was a sailor (or pirate) who stood either at the bow (at the front of the ship), or high above the ship's sails in what was called the "crow's nest."

The lookout had several jobs. He had to watch for any dangers to his own ship that might come from other ships in the area. If he was on a *merchant ship* (one which carried supplies and valuables from one seaport to another), he had to be on the look-out for pirates, who wanted to take the items his ship was trying to deliver. He also had to help keep watch for other things that might cause harm like jagged rocks in the water. Finally, he had to help the ship's captain and navigator find land when they approached the end of their voyage.

On a *pirate ship*, the lookout had to search for ships to attack and to watch out for Navy ships that might attack his own vessel.

Pretend you are being tested for the job of lookout, and have a look at the word-search puzzle on the facing page. At the bottom of the page is a list of names, words, and phrases having to do with pirates and life at sea. Find all of these words and names hidden in the big jumble of letters grouped together in the middle of the page, circle them and then mark them off on the list below. Find them all and become lookout on your ship!

Pirate and Maritime Phrase Word Puzzle

Find and circle the words, names and phrases listed at the bottom of this page in the puzzle below. This one may take a little more time to complete. Are you up to the challenge?

```
A B C D E F G H I J K L M N O P Q R S T U V W S C U R V Y W U T S R Q P O N S K U L L H
A L C D E F G H T R E A S U R E C H E S T V W X Y Z Y X E Y E P A T C H O N M L K J I H
D A V E Y J O N E S K L M N O P Q R S F U V W X Y Z Y X W V U T S R Q P B A M L K J I C
A C C D E F G H I J K L M N O P Q R S L U V W X Y Z Y X W V U T S R Q P O N M L K J I R
A K C D E F G H I J K L M N O P Q R S I U V W S Y R X W S T A R B O A R D M L K J M O
A B O O T Y G H I J K L M N S P Q R S N U V W X Y Z Y X W V U T S R Q P O N M L K J I S
S E C D E F G H I J K L M N O P Q L S T U V W X Y Z Y X W V U T S R Q P M R P L K J I S
H A C C A L I C O J A C K N I P C U T L A S S X Y Z Y X W V U T S R Q P O N M L K J I B
A R C D E I G H S J K L W N O P Q B S O O V I Y Z Y P O W D E R H O R N O N M L K J I O
N D C D E F G H I J K L M N I P Q B S C U V W X Y Z Y X P V U T S R Q P O N M L K J I N
T B C S E I G H I J K L S I O P M E S K U V W L O O T I R A T P R I V A T E E R K J R E
Y B C D E F G H I J K L M I O P Q R S T U V W X Y Z Y X E V U T S R Q P O N M L K J I S
M A R Y R E I D S J K L S N O P Q R S T U V W X Y Z Y X S V U S S S C A L L Y W A G I H
D A C B E F G H I J K L D A G G E R S T U V W X Y Z Y X M V U T S R Q P O N M L K J I H
X Y A Z E F G H I J K L M N O P Q R S T M V W P I E C E S O F E I G H T O N M A T E I H
B U C C A N E E R J K L M N O P Q R S T I V W X Y I Y X W V U D S R Q P O N M L K J I T
C A P T A I N K I D D L M N O P Q R S T U V W P R E S S W V U E S R Q P O N M L K J I A
A B C D M F G H S J K L T R I C O R N H A T W X Y M Y X W V U B S R Q P O N M L K J I N
P B C D E F G H I J K L M N O P Q R S T U V W X Y Z Y X W V U O S R Q P O N M L K J I K
E B C L O O K O U T K L I N O P Q R S A U V W X Y Z Y X W V U N S R Q P O N M L K J I A
G B C D E F G H S J K L S N O P Q R I L O L D S A L T X X M U N S R J O L L Y R O G E R
L B C Q U A R T E R D E C K O P M R S L U V W X Y Z Y X W V U E S R Q P O N M L K J I D
E B C D E F G H I J K L M N O P Q R S S C A B B A R D X W V U T S I Q P I N M L P R O W
G B C D E F G H I J K L M N O P Q R S H U V W X Y Z Y X W V U T S R Q P O P M L K J I H
A R M D M F M H M C O N S C R I P T I O N W X Y Z Y X W V U T S R Q P O L M P K J I R
S L O O K O U T I J K L M N O P Q R S P U V W X Y Z Y X W R U D D E R P O A M O K J I E
A B C D O F G H I J K L M A N N E B O N N Y W X Y Z Y X W V U T S R Q P O N M R K J I E
B E Q E F G H I J K L R U M P Q R S T U V W X Y Z Y X W L E E W A R D O K M T K J I F
```

Jolly Roger	Scabbard	Eye Patch	Treasure Chest	Rudder
Pirate	Booty	Peg Leg	Powder Horn	Reef
Blackbeard	Tricorn Hat	Plank	Skull	Quarter Deck
Tall Ship	Conscription	Port	Crossbones	Prow
Dagger	Pieces of Eight	Starboard	Davy Jones	Press
Flintlock	Lubber	Calico Jack	Shanty	Leeward
Cutlass	Stede Bonnet	Mary Reid	Scurvy	Mate
Rum	Privateer	Anne Bonny	Scallywag	Lookout
Tankard	Buccaneer	Captain Kidd	Old Salt	Loot

The solution to this puzzle is found on page 65

49

(For Parents)

Host Your

Own

Pirate

Party!

Helpful Hints

Whether it's for a birthday, school gathering, or to celebrate some other special event in a child's life, a pirate-themed party is a popular choice.

On the pages to follow, you'll find directions for making simple but fun newspaper pirate hats as well as suggestions for pirate-themed games, simple refreshments, and party supplies.

You'll also find ready-made invitation samples (all you have to do is copy one and add the party details on the reverse side).

Planning

As with any important project, the first step is planning what items are needed, how much time will be necessary to get tasks completed, and then setting aside enough time to insure everything gets done.

You can find a great many pirate and maritime-related novelties, decorations, costumes, and props either online or at your local party store. If you don't have time to make the things described on the pages to follow, but have the money to spend on ready-made items, a party store may well be your best bet. It's no secret that children are sometimes fickle creatures. Some will greatly appreciate the time and effort it takes to make party favors, treats, and costume pieces by hand. Others would be happier knowing that everything at the party is store-bought.

If you do want to make the items described over the next few pages, you may save a little cash, and you may find the experience of preparing things yourself personally more rewarding.

Along with directions on how to make pirate hats and suggestions for food to be shared at the your child's party, you'll also resources for the properties needed (*additional resources can be found on the publisher's website:* www.RealStoryBooks.com).

You can pick up inexpensive plastic giveaway items like coins, "jewels," and napkins at your local retail party store. Alternatively, you may elect to substitute items you already have for "treasure" pieces like old Mardi Gras coins, inexpensive bead necklaces and foil-covered candies from your local grocery store.

Invitations

Thanks to instant-printing technology and the Internet, it's now easy and often inexpensive to get customized party invitations with your child's name—and even his or her photo—printed on them.

It may be more fun, though, to manufacture your own invitations. Printing on parchment paper provides a more authentic look. Large chain arts and crafts supply stores, like Michaels and Hobby Lobby, sometimes carry a nice, aged-looking parchment paper manufactured by the *American Document Company*. You can also get less expensive parchment card stock and paper at most office supply stores, or you can create your own by soaking plain paper in tea overnight.

One invitation design example is shown here If you don't draw, you can make a photocopy of this image. More invitation designs are seen on the next page.

Invitation Sample One   G. Edmonds

Invitation Sample Two

Copy your choice of invitation design (for private use only, please). Write the details concerning for whom, where and when the party is to be give on the reverse (blank) side of the invitation.

Invitations should be presented two to three weeks in advance of the event.

Invitation Sample Three

Most young children will be excited to receive a genuine "message in a bottle." Plastic bottles can be sent through the mail uninsured. Glass bottles are best delivered in person.

Just remove the normal label from a smaller glass or plastic bottle (use a blow dryer, set on high heat, to loosen the adhesive), then replace it with one like that seen below. A thin layer of white glue (like *Elmer's*) will work, or you can secure the new label with tape. The party invitation is then rolled up, and left sticking slightly out of the bottle's top.

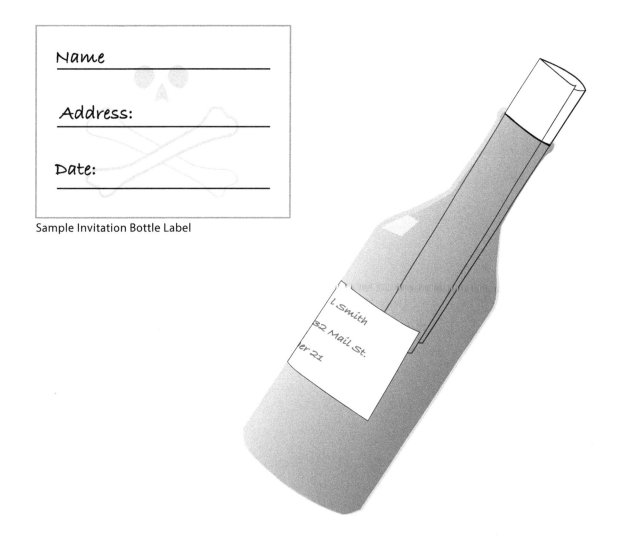

Name _____

Address: _____

Date: _____

Sample Invitation Bottle Label

How to Make a Pirate Hat

This classic "pirate hat" design is made from a sheet of newspaper or from similarly sized wrapping or craft paper. It takes only a few minutes to make several as party favors for your child's guests.

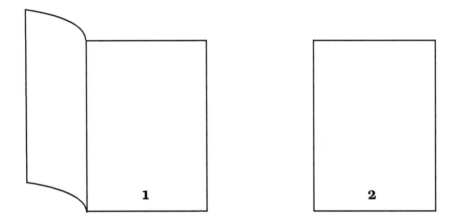

Begin by taking a large single sheet of newspaper (*not* tabloid sized) and folding it into it's normal closed condition (figures 1 and 2).

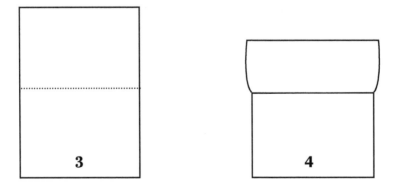

Next, fold over the top of the closed sheet so that it meets the bottom of the paper and then make a crease at the fold (figures 3 and 4).

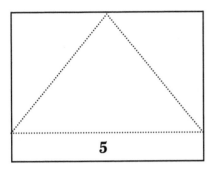

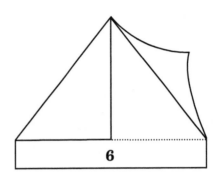

Fold down the upper corners of the folded sheet down, toward you, into equal-sized triangular shapes, one at a time, as illustrated in figures 5 and 6. Leave an inch or so at the bottom free.

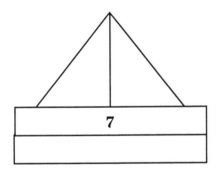

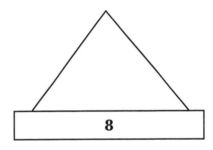

Fold the outermost rectangular section at the bottom up, toward you, as seen in figure 7. Flip the hat over and fold *up* the last rectangular piece as shown in figure 8. Open up the at the hat at the bottom, as seen in figure 9 and you're all set. If desired, you may paint the finished hat.

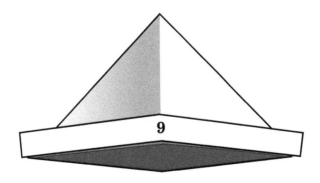

Party Treats

If you've ever been to a high school football game, you've probably heard *"two bits, four bits, six bits, a dollar -- all for* [the home team] *stand up and holler!"* The first part of this expression came from a coin that was in common use in the Western hemisphere hundreds of years ago. The Spanish Dollar Coins (known as "pieces-of-eight") were among the items commonly stolen by pirates. They were cut into eight pieces and spent that way. Made of solid silver, the individual coin sections were weighed to determine their value.

Even in the early to mid-20th Century, it was common for people to use the expression "two bits" when referring to a quarter-dollar coin.

On the facing page is a design very similar to the original *"Real de a Ocho"*(Spanish Dollar) coin. Of course, the words on the outside ring originally appeared in Spanish (and in Latin as the coin began being copied by other countries, including the early American colonies).

If you have cake-decorating skills, you can copy this basic design and substitute the birthday child's name for the original wording. The cake has only a single layer and is baked in a large cake pan (follow the directions on your cake mix box or use your own favorite recipe).

The finished cake can be covered with icing and sprinkled with decorative silver candy glitter (available at most grocery stores). As you cut the cake into eight pieces you explain what the coins were, and how they were used. Each child gets a piece along with a scoop of ice cream.

Party Treats

HAPPY BIRTHDAY TO

BIRTHDAY CHILD'S NAME

"Pieces of Eight" Birthday Cake Design

Party Treats

Additional party treats might include the popular chocolate "coins" covered in gold foil. These, and plastic "pirate" coins, are available by mail (and online) from *The Oriental Trading Company* or from your local party or discount retailer. Add to these some large jelly beans (representing "gemstones") and a couple of other pirate-related small toy items and you'll have additional sweet treats for the party-goers.

A cardboard box can be painted and decorated as a "treasure chest" and each child can use a large spoon (or a small-sized plastic beach shovel) to scoop out a portion of the goodies for themselves.

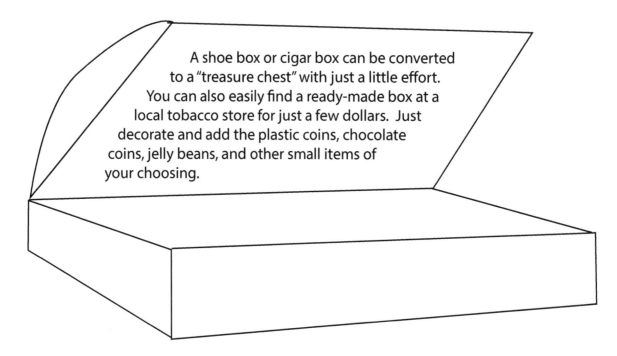

A shoe box or cigar box can be converted to a "treasure chest" with just a little effort. You can also easily find a ready-made box at a local tobacco store for just a few dollars. Just decorate and add the plastic coins, chocolate coins, jelly beans, and other small items of your choosing.

It's always a great idea to offer some healthier food options for both children and adults at your child's party. Vegetable trays, cheese and cracker packages, and healthy vegetable dips are popular choices.

Games & Party Favors

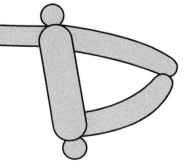

Visit **The REAL Story of Pirates** book page on our publisher's website: *RealStoryBooks.com,* to find simple video instructions for making balloon pirate swords for your party. You'll find other pirate-related activities and resources there as well, at the bottom of the page.

Please keep in mind that balloons of *any* kind are not appropriate for children under the age of four because they can pose a potential choking hazard for the very young.

Fun party games for the kids can include an indoor or outdoor treasure hunt in which plastic gold coins or other small items are hidden in not-too-hard-to-find places.

A homemade eye patch is always popular with kids. Make it from either stiff fabric or a piece thin tape-covered cardboard. Metallic-gold plastic coins will be "treasured" as a take-home gift.

A lawn ring (or small beanbag) toss are popular with younger children, too. Decorate the playing surfaces with pirate-related images like the eye patch, Jolly Roger, or similar themes. Although walking the plank was not a common practice, most children enjoy pretending it was in a shallow backyard or community pool, at summer parties.

Treasure Maze
SOLUTION

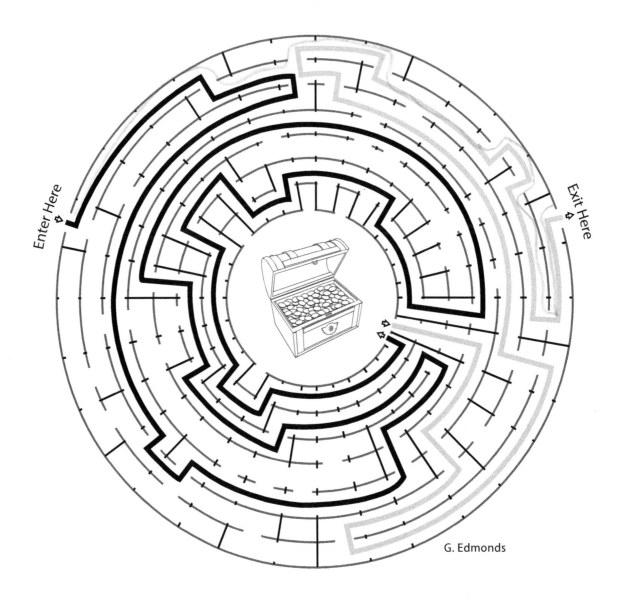

Enter Here

Exit Here

G. Edmonds

Follow the dark-gray line to get to the treasure chest in the center of the maze.
Follow the light gray line to find your way out.

Fact or Tall Tale?
True or False Quiz Answers

1. True. John "Bartholomew" (Black Bart) Roberts never steered far from his Christian roots. He is said to have regularly conducted church services for members of his crew on Sunday mornings, and he never consumed drinks containing alcohol. He was the first to create a "pirate's code," which was meant to insure that all men and women in a pirate crew were treated fairly and given equal voting rights.

2. True. For a time, it was common practice for pirate ships to forcibly enlist members of a captured ship's crew to serve as pirates on their own ships. If the crew members refused, they faced death or might be abandon at sea.

3. False. There are very few (if any) verified cases of a person forced being to "walk the plank" as punishment. If it happened at all, the practice was extremely rare. There were, however, on both pirate and Naval vessels, even worse punishments for those who misbehaved or who refused to cooperate. Among these was "keel hauling," in which a victim was bound in ropes and dragged underwater along the bottom of a moving ship. Another punishment was to beaten or "flogged" with a whip or an instrument called a "cat-o-nine-tails." These cruel punishments often ended in the death of the person being punished.

4. *True*. Accustomed to living aboard a ship that was constantly being tossed around in the sea, a mariner got used to putting his elbows on the table to keep his food from sliding off. Those looking to kidnap sailors would look for men with their elbows on the table in pubs, recognizing that they were experienced seaman. "Lubbers," or people who lived and worked on land, were left alone.

5. *False*. Although it was common practice for pirates to split up stolen property (according to the pirate's code), they almost never buried their treasures in the sand. This may be because the stolen items were often perishable things like food, spices, and wine.

6. *True*. Aboard every ship (pirate or otherwise), there were navigators who had to be able to recognize the major constellations, stars, and planets in the night sky. They used these as "landmarks" to guide the ship.

7. *True*. Scurvy, caused by a lack of Vitamin C, occurred because fresh fruit and vegetables were rare aboard ships. The British Royal Navy (and pirates) began serving a mixture of rum and water to sailors to keep the crew happy. Limes were sometimes stored, and their juice added to the mix to help prevent scurvy. This old practice led to British sailors being called "Limeys" (which was considered an offensive term) by mariners from other nations.

Word Puzzle SOLUTION

A B C D E F G H I J K L M N O P Q R S T U V W S C U R V Y W U T S R Q P O N S K U L L H
A L C D E F G H T R E A S U R E C H E S T V W X Y Z Y X E Y E P A T C H O N M L K J I H
D A V E Y J O N E S K L M N O P Q R S F U V W X Y Z Y X W V U T S R Q P B A M L K J I C
A C C D E F G H I J K L M N O P Q R S L U V W X Y Z Y X W V U T S R Q P O N M L K J I R
A K C D E F G H I J K L M N O P Q R S I U V W S Y R X W S T A R B O A R D M L K J M O
A B O O T Y G H I J K L M N S P Q R S N U V W X Y Z Y X W V U T S R Q P O N M L K J I S
S E C D E F G H I J K L M N O P O L S T U V W X Y Z Y X W V U T S R Q P M R P L K J I S
H A C C A L I C O J A C K N I P C U T L A S S X Y Z Y X W V U T S R Q P O N M L K J I B
A R C D E I G H S J K L W N O P Q B S O O V I Y Z Y P O W D E R H O R N O N M L K J I O
N D C D E F G H I J K L M N I P Q B S C U V W X Y Z Y X P V U T S R Q P O N M L K J I N
T B C S E I G H I J K L S I O P M E S K U V W L O O T R A T P R I V A T E E R K J R E
Y B C D E F G H I J K L M I O P Q R S T U V W X Y Z Y X E V U T S R Q P O N M L K J I S
M A R Y R E I D S J K L S N O P Q R S T U V W X Y Z Y X S V U S S S C A L L Y W A G I H
D A C P I R A T E K L D A G G E R S T U V W X Y Z Y X M V U T S R Q P O N M L K J I H
X Y A Z E F G H I J K L M N O P Q R S T M V W P I E C E S O F E I G H T O N M A T E H
B U C C A N E E R J K L M N O P Q R S T I V W X Y I Y X W V U D S R Q P O N M L K J I T
C A P T A I N K I D D L M N O P Q R S T U V W P R E S S W V U E S R Q P O N M L K J I A
A B C D M F G H S J K L T R I C O R N H A T W X Y M Y X W V U B S R Q P O N M L K J I N
P B C D E F G H I J K L M N O P Q R S T U V W X Y Z Y X W V U O S R Q P O N M L K J I K
E B C L O O K O U T K L I N O P Q R S A U V W X Y Z Y X W V U N S R Q P O N M L K J I A
G B C D E F G H S J K L S N O P Q R I L O L D S A L T X X M U N S R J O L L Y R O G E R
L B C Q U A R T E R D E C K O P M R S L U V W X Y Z Y X W V U E S R Q P O N M L K J I D
E B C D E F G H I J K L M N O P Q R S S C A B B A R D X W V U T S I Q P I N M L P R O W
G B C D E F G H I J K L M N O P Q R S H U V W X Y Z Y X W V U T S R Q P O P M L K J I H
A R M D M F M H M C O N S C R I P T I O N W X Y Z Y X W V U T S R Q P O L M P K J I R
S L O O K O U T I J K L M N O P Q R S P U V W X Y Z Y X W R U D D E R P O A M O K J I E
A B C D O F G H I J K L M A N N E B O N N Y W X Y Z Y X W V U T S R Q P O N M R K J I E
B E Q E F G H I J K L R U M P Q R S T U V W X Y Z Y X W L E E W A R D O K M T K J I F

Jolly Roger	Scabbard	Eye Patch	Treasure Chest	Rudder
Pirate	Booty	Peg Leg	Powder Horn	Reef
Blackbeard	Tricorn Hat	Plank	Skull	Quarter Deck
Tall Ship	Conscription	Port	Crossbones	Prow
Dagger	Pieces of Eight	Starboard	Davy Jones	Press
Flintlock	Lubber	Calico Jack	Shanty	Leeward
Cutlass	Stede Bonnet	Mary Reid	Scurvy	Mate
Rum	Privateer	Anne Bonny	Scallywag	Lookout
Tankard	Buccaneer	Captain Kidd	Old Salt	Loot

❧Glossary (a list of pirate-related words)

Aft: The back or rearmost part of a boat or ship.

Ale: A drink containing alcohol, like beer. People often drank beer or ale even on land in pirate days because local water supplies were contaminated.

Aye: A mariner's word for "yes."

Backstaff: A wooden navigation instrument used to measure the level of objects in the sky.

Boat: A vehicle used for transportation on the water, a boat is smaller than a ship.

Booty: Another word for treasure or stolen goods.

Bosun: Also spelled "Boatswain," a person on the ship in charge of the crew, as in a "Petty Officer."

Bounty: The reward offered for capturing or killing a pirate. Also the name of a famous ship whose crew mutinied against the officers.

Bow: The front of a boat or ship (rhymes with "how").

Buccaneer: Another word for pirate.

Code: Code can mean several things, but to pirates, the "code" was a special set of rules that everyone agreed to follow.

Compass: A navigation tool with a magnetic needle which always points north.

Conscription: A word that means to *press* (or force) sailors into serving in the Navy or another branch of the military—to be drafted, in modern language.

Crew: The men (and sometimes women) who work together as a team on a boat or ship.

Cutlass: A sword with a curved blade that is sharp on both edges.

Dagger: A short knife with a sharp point used as a weapon for throwing or stabbing.

Ebb: The movement of the ocean tide out to sea.

Fleet: A collection of ships belonging to a company or sovereign nation's Navy.

Flintlock: A kind of firearm using black powder (*gunpowder*) to fire a metal ball at a target or enemy.

Flow: The movement of the ocean tide toward the shore—the opposite of "Ebb."

Galleon: A very large Spanish merchant vessel or military ship.

Hatch: A door on a ship leading from one deck or compartment to another.

Hatchet: A small ax used as a weapon or tool.

Jib: The front or foremost sail on a boat or ship.

Keel: The bottom-most part of a boat or ship that should always remain under water.

Knots: The unit used to measure the speed of a ship on the water.

Lee: The side of a ship or boat that the wind is blowing against is called the Lee side (or *Windward Side*).

Line: A length of rope being used to tie something to something else on a ship.

Loot: Items stolen from a ship or land property that is kept by a pirate. The word also means the act or process of stealing.

Aye: A mariner's word for "yes."

Lubber: The name given by mariners to people who only live and work on the shore (land).

Mariner: Another word for sailor, or someone who lives and works on the sea.

Mate: A friend or fellow worker on a ship.

Mutiny: The act of taking a ship from its captain and (sometimes) other officers. Mutineers very frequently went on to become pirates.

Peg: A stump or bit of carved wood, sometimes used to replace missing body parts, as in a *peg leg*.

Perishable: An item like food or wine that would rot or go bad in a short period of time if not stored.

Pirate: A sailor who makes his living as a thief.

Plank: A fairly long and wide piece of wood used to climb aboard and exit a ship. Pirates did *not* often make people "walk the plank" into the ocean.

Port: The side of a ship on the left, as the ship travels forward in the water.

Press: In mariner's language, to be pressed meant that you were forced to serve on a ship, against your will—see also *Conscription*.

Privateer: A sailor who was hired by a government or company to work as a pirate.

Reef: An underwater outcropping of rocks or other hard objects that could damage a ship's keel.

Rum: A popular drink containing a lot of alcohol.

Prow: The leading edge at the bow of the ship.

Sailor: A person who sails or works on a ship at sea, same as a *Mariner*.

Scabbard: A leather sheath or sleeve that protects and holds a sword or knife.

Scurvy: A disease often suffered by sailors because their diets lacked Vitamin C.

Shanty: A small poorly-built shack on land or a song sung by sailors - also called a *Sea Shanty*.

Ship: An ocean-going vessel that is large enough to contain a boat, a boat cannot contain a ship.

Starboard: The opposite of **Port**, or the right side of the ship as you face forward.

Swab: To clean a ship, as with a mop, also an offensive name to call a sailor.

Swell: A hill or mountain of water moving across the surface of the ocean, waves travel on top of swells.

Vessel: Another word for ship, or an object that can contain something else.

About the Author

Gregory Edmonds has worked as a journalist, illustrator, and editor of newspapers, books, and magazines in the academic and entertainment worlds since the 1970s. He is a former police public information officer and was for decades—with his business partner Lyle Brite—a part-time professional illusionist. He was inducted into the International Brotherhood of Magicians' "Order of Merlin" in 1999.

Greg and his wife Tammie (also an artist who creates sterling silver jewelry and textile pieces) have two grown children, Alex and Mary. As this book is published, they share their lives and home with a pair of mixed-breed 12-year-old dogs named Sadie and Trouble.

In addition to writing and creating illustrations for books and magazines, Greg enjoys painting portraits of people, pets, and wildlife subjects, and assisting animal welfare organizations.

He is interested in unusual and mysterious practices and beliefs of different cultures now and in the

Greg Edmonds, author and illustrator

past and he sometimes consults with other authors and publishers as a contributing editor for books related to the history of magic.

The REAL Story of Pirates is the first in a planned series of factual reading, discussion, and activity books for young people (and interested grown-ups) on a variety of popular subjects. Future books will range in topics from dinosaurs to doctors and from Halloween to the history of space flight. Greg also writes biographical and historical works for adult readers.